Smart Alec's

Spooky Jokes

I DON'T BELIEVE IN GHOSTS

Smart Alec's

SPOOKY JOKES for Kids

Illustrated by
D. Mostyn

CLIVEDEN PRESS

Copyright © 1991 Cliveden Press.
All rights reserved.
Published by Cliveden Press,
An Egmont Company, Egmont House,
PO Box 111, Great Ducie Street,
Manchester M60 3BL.
Printed in Italy.
ISBN 0 7498 0381 9

spooky

What kind of spook can you hold on the tip of your finger?
  A bogey!

Did the bionic monster have a brother?
  No, but he had a lot of trans-sisters.

1st Undertaker: I've just been given the sack.
2nd Undertaker: Why?
1st Undertaker: I buried someone in the wrong grave.
2nd Undertaker: That was a grave mistake.

Spook: Should you eat spiders and slugs and zombie slime on an empty stomach?
Witch: No, you should eat them on a plate.

GHOSTLY UGH!

FLICK THIS CORNER OF YOUR BOOK
THROUGH FROM THE BACK AND SEE
SMART ALEC OUTSMARTED BY BLACKIE
THE MONSTER. IT'S HAUNTING!

Did you hear about the phantom who ate the Christmas tree decorations? He died of tinselitis.

How do you get a ghost to lie perfectly flat?
  You use a spirit level.

Did you hear about Sid the spook? He got drunk so often he was known as the methylated spirit.

What's Count Dracula's favourite breakfast?
  Readyneck.

A hairdresser, a carpenter and a lollipop lady were out for a ramble in the forest one day when they got lost. Night fell and they all became alarmed as they stumbled through the trees, not knowing where they were going. At last, in a clearing, they spotted a little shack, its lights glowing an eerie blue colour in the moonlight. 'Shelter!' cried the hairdresser. 'Let's go in,' said the carpenter. 'It looks a bit creepy to me,' warned the lollipop lady. 'You two go in first.' So in went the hairdresser – and came face to face with an ugly old witch.

'What do you do for a living?' she asked.

'I'm a hairdresser,' he said. And so she took a pair of scissors and cut off all his toes.

The next one in was the carpenter. 'What do you do for a living?' the witch asked. 'I'm a carpenter,' he replied. And so she took out a saw and sawed all his toes off, one by one.

Finally the lollipop lady, who had been listening all the time, came in very nervously. 'I'm a lollipop lady,' she said very defiantly. 'So you'd better suck all *my* toes off!'

Woman in bed: Aaagh! Aaaagh! A ghost just floated into my room!
Ghost: Don't worry, madam, I'm just passing through.

On which side does a monster have most of its fur?

The outside.

1st Witch: Two of my pet spiders just got married.
2nd Witch: Really?
1st Witch: Yes – it's so nice to have newly-webs around.

Who got higher marks in the History exam – Smart Alec or the prehistoric monster?

The prehistoric monster. He passed with extinction.

Did you hear about the horrible hairy monster who did farmyard impressions? He didn't do the noises, he just made the smells.

What do you call a witch who drives very badly?

A road hag.

What was Dr Jekyll's favourite game?

Hyde and Seek.

There once was a ghost from Darjeeling
Who got on a train bound for Ealing
It said at the door
'Please don't sit on the floor'
So he floated up and sat on the ceiling.

*What's the difference between Beethoven and a
dead body?*
   One composes and the other decomposes.

How does Dracula keep fit?
   He plays batminton.

*'Waiter, waiter,' called a diner at the Monster
Café. 'There's a hand in my soup.'*
   'That's not your soup, sir, that's your finger
   bowl.'

Where do undertakers go when they retire?
  Gravesend.

What do you get if you cross a ghost, a helpful boy and a vegetable?
  An invisible Brussels sprout.

1st Monster: My boyfriend says I have cheeks like peaches and ears like petals.
2nd Monster: Yes, football 'peaches' and bicycle 'pedals'.

If a flying saucer is an aircraft, does that make a flying broomstick a witchcraft?

Dr Frankenstein: We won't be cold this winter! I've just crossed a sheep with a porcupine.
Igor: And what did you get?
Dr Frankenstein: An animal that knits its own sweaters.

What did Tarzan say when he saw the monsters coming?
    Here come the monsters.
And what did he say when he saw the monsters coming with sunglasses on?
    Nothing – he didn't recognize them.

How can you tell if a vampire has a glass eye?
    It usually comes out in conversation.

A monster who came from Devizes
Had noses of different sizes.
One was so small
It was no use at all –
But the other won several prizes.

What do you get if you cross a ghost with a packet of crisps?
   Snacks that go crunch in the night.

Why did the werewolf cross the road?
   Because the chicken was on holiday.

What's white, built on sleek lines, and beats other spooks from a standing start?
   A turbo-charged phantom.

A flute player was walking home late one night from a concert. He took a short cut through the local woods, and he hadn't gone far before he bumped into a ghost and then a vampire. Pulling out his flute he began to play a lovely trilling melody – and the ghost and the vampire stood entranced. Soon the musician was surrounded by a crowd of phantoms and monsters and goblins and cannibals and witches listening to the music. Then up bounded a werewolf. 'Yum! Yum!' he growled, and he gobbled up the flute player.
   'Why did you do that?' complained the others. 'We were enjoying it.'
   'Eh, what was that?' said the werewolf.

What do mermaids eat for breakfast?
  Mermalade.

1st Witch: What's your black cat's name?
2nd Witch: Dunno, he won't tell me.

What do you call a monster with gravy, meat and potatoes on his head?
  Stew.

Why is it so difficult to become a coroner?
  You have to take stiff exams.

The villagers of Lower Bumpstead were going on a Midsummer picnic, but unfortunately they forgot to invite the elderly lady who was believed by some to be a witch. On the morning of the picnic the vicar suddenly realized what had happened and went to invite her to come along.

'No thanks,' said the old lady. 'I've already cast my spells, and I don't want to get soaked or attacked by a swarm of bees.'

Dracula: Have you seen the new monster from Poland?
Frankenstein: A Pole?
Dracula: Yes – you can tell him by his wooden expression.

1st Witch: Beer cans, old newspapers, lolly sticks, orange juice cartons . . .
2nd Witch: Shut up, you're talking rubbish again.

Why did Dr Frankenstein have his telephone cut off?
Because he wanted to win the Nobel prize.

Why does Count Dracula sleep in a coffin?
Because the council won't give him a flat.

What do phantom football supporters sing?
Here we ghost, here we ghost, here we ghost!

Did you hear about the monster with one eye
at the back of his head and one at the front?
He was terribly moody because he couldn't
see eye to eye with himself.

Lady Jane Grey
Had nothing to say.
What could she have said
After losing her head?

Who wrote Count Dracula's life story?
  The ghost writer.

What did his friends call Yorrick at school?
  Numbskull.

Rumours that Count Dracula is about to
marry Glenda the Ghoul are not true. They're
just good fiends, that's all.

What should you give short elves?
  Elf-raising flour.

Do werewolves always snore?
  Only when they're asleep.

What do Egyptian monsters put on their toenails?
  Nile varnish.

Where does Dracula keep his savings?
  In the blood bank.

Why are werewolves such good comedians?
  They make people howl with laughter.

How do you know when there's a monster hiding under your bed?
  When you wake up your nose is squashed against the ceiling.

Old Ghost: I'm going to give up haunting.
Young Ghost: Why?
Old Ghost: I don't seem to frighten people any more. I might as well be alive for all they care.

Two little boys went scrumping for apples one evening and were chased by the owner of the orchard. They ran into a graveyard just as it was getting dark and hid behind a gravestone. One of the boys dropped his apples and two of them rolled over towards the gate. 'We'll pick them up on the way out,' he said. 'While we're waiting for it to get really dark, let's divide the apples between us.'

It just so happened that an old lady was taking a short cut across the graveyard that night, and as she passed the gravestone she heard a little voice saying, 'That's one for you and one for me, one for you and one for me . . .' In terror she ran to the gate and into the arms of a passing gentleman.

'Help!' she cried. 'There are ghosts in the graveyard and they're dividing up the bodies!' Nervously they stepped back into the cemetary. And through the darkness came a whispering voice, 'There's one for you and one for me. Oh, and don't forget those two over by the gate . . .'

Ghost: How do you do?
Spook: How do you do what?

What did the boy monster squid say to the girl monster squid?
    'I want to hold your hand, your hand, your hand . . .'

Why are old ghosts boring?
    Because they're groan-ups.

Vampire: You know, they say blood is thicker than water!
Victim: So what? So is porridge!

What is the best-selling cannibal book?
  'How to Serve Your Fellow Man'

Monster Mum: Did you put the cat out?
Little Monster: Was it on fire again?

Why did the wooden monsters stand in a circle?
  They were having a board meeting.

Dr Frankenstein decided to build an extension to his laboratory, so he crossed a cement mixer, a ghoul and a chicken. Now he's got a demon bricklayer.

What did the angry monster do when he got his gas bill?
   He exploded.

A boy monster and a girl monster were out on their first date. Despite being very shy, things seemed to be going well, and they went for a drive in the boy monster's lorry. Suddenly he stopped. 'Shall I show you where I had my operation?' he asked.
   'All right,' stammered the girl monster.
   'Right,' said the boy monster starting the lorry, 'it's second left at the traffic lights and straight down the high street.'

1st Monster: Where do fleas go in winter?
Werewolf: Search me!

1st Witch: I like your toad. He always has such a nice expression on his face.
2nd Witch: Yes, he is nice. It's because he's a hoptimist.

I'M NOT A TOAD! I'M A FROGGIE

Where does the Sandman keep his sleeping sand?

In his knapsack.

A monster walked into a shop selling dress fabrics and said, 'I'd like 6 metres of pink satan for my wife.'

'It's *satin*, sir, not satan,' said the assistant. 'Satan is something that looks like the devil.'

'Oh,' said the monster, 'you know my wife?'

Frankenstein: Help, I've got a short circuit!
Igor: Don't worry, I'll lengthen it.

What did the smelly monster say when the wind changed?

It's all coming back to me now.

Smart Alec: Our school is haunted!
Silly Billy: Really?
Smart Alec: Yes, the head teacher's always talking about the school spirit.

What is a skeleton?
　Someone who went on a diet and forgot to say 'when'.

Ugly Monster: I got 150 Valentine cards last year.
Witch: That's amazing!
Ugly Monster: Yes, it is. The only problem was that I couldn't afford to post them all.

Where do monster stingrays come from?
　Stingapore.

A big monster went to the pictures and sat in front of a little boy. 'Can you see?' asked the monster.

'No I can't,' said the boy.

'Well,' said the monster. 'Just watch me and laugh when I do.'

How can you tell when you're in bed with Count Dracula?

He has a big D on his pyjamas.

Smart Alec: Do you know that there's a monster in disguise hiding up every oak tree?
Silly Billy: That's ridiculous.
Smart Alec: Have you ever seen one?
Silly Billy: Certainly not.
Smart Alec: That just shows how well it works!

Have you heard about the mad monster comedian?

He kept trying to joke people to death.

1st Witch: Why are you using a goldfish to cast your spells?
2nd Witch: I can't afford a black cat.

Did you hear about the Irish monster who built a wooden car? Wooden seats, wooden engine, wooden wheels. The only problem was, it wooden go.

What's grey and hairy and can see just as well from either end?
   A werewolf with its eyes closed.

Monsters are so romantic. Did you hear about the one who bought his wife a fur coat for her birthday?
He gave her two steel traps and a shotgun.

What was written on the bionic monster's gravestone?
    Rust in peace.

What do you call a short vampire?
    A pain in the knee.

What are the posh giant's favourite pastimes?
    Haunting, shooting and fishing.

Why did the monster buy a sledgehammer?
    To burst his spots.

1st Monster: I've been working so hard at terrorising people I feel half dead!
2nd Monster: Shall I arrange for you to be buried up to your waist?

1st Ghost: Who's that walking down the street?
2nd Ghost: The invisible man.
1st Ghost: He looks like a real wally.
2st Ghost: Don't be rotten – can't you see he's not all there?

Where do Red Indian ghosts live?
  In creepy tepees.

How did the witch's frog die?
  It Kermitted suicide.

Werewolf: The Bride of Frankenstein has a lovely face.
Ghost: Only if you read between the lines.

Seen in the local newspaper:
THE ANNUAL MEETING OF THE
CLAIRVOYANTS CIRCLE HAS HAD TO
BE CANCELLED DUE TO UNFORESEEN
CIRCUMSTANCES.

What did the monster say when he saw Smart Alec asleep in bed?
   'Yum yum! Breakfast in bed . . .'

What comes out at night and goes 'Munch, munch, ouch!'
   A vampire with a rotten tooth.

A short, fat, hairy monster was waiting for a train and decided to while away the time by weighing himself on a machine on the station platform. Once he'd weighed himself he looked at the chart that indicated the ideal weight for each height.
   'Having any problems?' asked another passenger. 'Are you overweight?'
   'No,' said the monster, 'I'm just four feet too short.'

*What should you do if a ghost comes in
through the front door?*
　　Run out through the back door.

Dracula: Why did Igor lose his job?
Monster: Illness.
Dracula: Anything serious?
Monster: Dr Frankenstein got sick of him.

Did you hear about the absent-minded
monster who went round and round in a
revolving door for three hours?
He didn't know if he was coming or going.

If you're a regular at the Monster Café you'll
know that it isn't famous for either the quality
or flavour of its food. Only the other day a
vampire called the waiter over.
　　'Is this coffee or tea?' he asked. 'It's
disgusting – it tastes like disinfectant.'
　　'In that case it's tea,' said the waiter. 'Our
coffee tastes like paraffin.'

Ghost Postman: Is this letter for you? The name's smudged.
Ghost: No, my name's George Ghastly.

Witch: I'm going crazy!
Monster: Why?
Witch: The werewolves next door have just had a baby, and it howls all night.

Phantom: You know, there are some kinds of monster which have never been seen.
Spook: Yes, like yetis.
Phantom: Hasn't anybody seen one?
Spook: Not yeti.

How does a ghost count to ten?
   One, boo, three, four, five, six, seven, hate, nine, frighten!

Are Igor and Dr Frankenstein much fun at parties?
   Yes, they keep everyone in stitches.

Mother Vampire: The shame! How can I face the neighbours?

Monster: What's happened?

Mother Vampire: A zombie just tripped over in the playground and my boy Vince fainted at the sight of blood!

Why do ghosts like living in tall buildings?
   Because they have lots of scarecases.

Smart Alec: If you don't believe in ghosts I dare you to spend a night in the haunted house.

Silly Billy: No, I *don't* believe in ghosts, but I might be wrong.

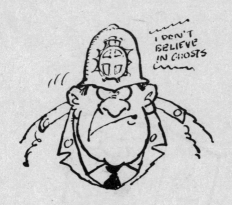

Why do monsters find it difficult to swallow vicars?
   Because you can't keep a good man down.

Zombie: Where does your Mum come from?
Abominable Snowman: Alaska.
Zombie: Don't worry, I'll ask her myself.

What kind of cake do monsters hate most?
   Cakes of soap.

Did you hear about the vampire comedian?
He swalled an Oxo cube and made a laughing stock of himself.

Why did the monster have his sundial floodlit?
  So that he could tell the time at night.

What's black and bounces?
  A rubber witch.

Mrs Monster: My son drank a tin of lighter fuel yesterday.
Mrs Ghost: What happened?
Mrs Monster: He ran up and down the stairs fifty times, flew around the front room, raced into the kitchen and went bang slap into the washing machine.
Mrs Ghost: Was he dead?
Mrs Monster: No, he just ran out of petrol.

Two monsters were brought up in court for fighting in the street. 'It was self-defence,' said the pink monster. 'The blue monster bit half my ear off.'
  The magistrate wasn't impressed. 'You are bound over to keep the peace for a year,' he thundered to the blue monster.
  'Oh, your honour, I can't do that,' he cried. 'I threw it away.'

Spook: What does coincidence mean?
Phantom: Funny, I was just going to ask you that.

Why did the monster eat yeast and shoe polish?
  He wanted to rise and shine.

Monster: Doctor, I swallowed a clock last night.
Dr Frankenstein: This could be serious – why didn't you come to see me earlier?
Monster: I didn't want to cause any alarm.

What did the headless coachman say when the green giant asked to borrow some money?
  Sorry, I'm a bit short.

A monster who lived in Penzance
Ate a small boy and two of his aunts.
A cat and a calf,
A pig and a half –
And now he can't button his pants.

*What did the three monsters play in the back of
the Mini Metro?*
   Squash.

1st Cannibal: I'm going to become a
vegetarian.
2nd Cannibal: Why?
1st Cannibal: You can go off people, you
know.

Mrs Monster: Did you hear what happened to
my son?
Mrs Spook: No – what?
Mrs Monster: He fell into a liquidizer.
Mrs Spook: Oh dear, he always was a crazy
mixed-up kid.

Werewolf: Werewolves are smarter than ghosts, you know.
Ghost: I never knew that.
Werewolf: See what I mean?

What's the best way of warding off ghostly doctors?
   Always carry an apple with you.

Witch: I've never been so insulted in my life! I went to a Hallowe'en party and at midnight they asked me to take my mask off.
Spook: Why are you so angry?
Witch: I wasn't wearing a mask.

Did you hear about the monster who ate little bits of metal every night?
It was his staple diet.

Smart Alec: Yesterday I took my girlfriend to see *Maggie the Monster's Revenge*.
Silly Billy: What was she like?
Smart Alec: Oh, 8 feet tall with two heads, green hair, a bolt through her necks . . .
Silly Billy: I meant your *girlfriend* . . .

What do you call a monster moth with a wingspan of 20 feet?
   A mam-moth.

What did the shy pebble monster say?
   I wish I was a little boulder.

Why did the turb-charged robot get stiff joints?
   He had vroomatism.

Who did the vampire marry?
  The girl necks door.

Why did the bald monster hang out of windows?
  To get some fresh 'air.

What's pink and grey and wrinkly and old and belongs to Grandpa monster?
  Grandmother monster.

Frankenstein's Monster: Did you like the dictionary I gave you for Christmas?
Dracula: Yes – I simply can't find words to thank you.

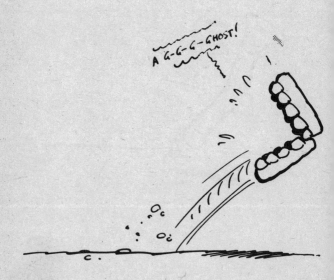

Once upon a time there was a bald ghost-hunter who went to stay for the night in the Haunted House. After dinner he went up to the Creepy Bedroom, where a terrifying ghost had been reported. He changed into his pyjamas, brushed his teeth, climbed into bed and then took off the wig he always wore and hung it on the bedpost. Then he settled down for a really spooky night. But by midnight the ghost still hadn't materialized and he dropped off to sleep.

'Some haunted house,' he grumbled when he woke up the following morning. 'I haven't slept so well for years.' He reached out automatically for his wig on the bedpost and was just about to put it on without thinking when he noticed something extremely odd – the wig had turned snowy white . . .

Why do undertakers go to the Earl's Court Exhibition Centre each year?
For the Hearse of the Year Show.

Why did the little monster do so well in his exams?
Because three heads are better than one.

What do short-sighted phantoms wear?
Spooktacles.

Why should you always be calm and polite when you meet cannibals?
There's no point in getting into a stew, is there?

Dr Frankenstein: How are fangs, Dracula?
Dracula: Not too good – I'm 50 litres overdrawn at the blood bank.

Heavenly Father, bless us,
And keep us all alive.
There's three of us for dinner –
We'll be cooked at half-past five. .

Do ghosts like going horseriding?
Yes, they're very fond of ghoulloping.

*How much did the psychiatrist charge
Frankenstein's monster for his first visit?*
    £20 for consultation
    £50 to repair the doorway
    £200 for a new couch

*What do you call a phantom with a frankfurter
on its head?*
    A head banger.

*On what day of the week do monsters eat
people?*
    Chewsdays.

Who won the monster beauty contest?
    No one.

1st Monster: I went to the circus last night.
2nd Monster: So did I. What did you think of the knife-throwing act?
1st Monster: I thought it was boring. He threw twenty knives at that soppy girl and missed every time.

Did you hear about the phantom who was engaged to a monster? When she found that he had a wooden leg – she broke it off, of course.

Define a very loud noise.
A skeleton dancing on a roof.

A little monster came home from school in tears. 'What's wrong?' asked his mother.

'It's the children at school,' he sobbed. 'They keep calling me big head.'

'Don't take any notice of them,' said his mother. 'They're only jealous. Would you go and do some shopping for me? We need five pounds of potatoes, two pounds of sugar, six apples, six oranges, two loaves and a dozen eggs.'

'All right,' said the little monster. 'But where is the shopping basket?'

'The handles are broken, dear, but don't worry. Just use your school cap instead.'

Smart Alec: I wish I had enough money to buy a huge monster.
Silly Billy: Why do you want a monster?
Smart Alec: I don't – I just want that much money.

Did you hear about the two monster frogs who went into a restaurant together? One of them ordered lunch but the other just sat silently. Eventually the other frog turned to him and said, 'What's wrong? Don't you want any lunch?'

'I'm sorry,' whispered the frog, 'but I've got a man in my throat.'

Why did the undertaker chop all his corpses into little bits?
Because he liked them to rest in pieces.

Did you hear about the short-sighted monster who fell in love with a piano?
It had such wonderful white teeth, how could he resist it?

Skeleton: I'm never going to a party again.
Monster: Why, what happened?
Skeleton: I went to one last night and people kept hanging their coats on me.

1st Monster: Every time we meet, you remind me of a famous film star.
2nd Monster: Meryl Streep? Madonna? Raquel Welch?
1st Monster: No, E.T.

Why did Nelson's ghost wear a three-cornered hat?
  To keep his three-cornered head warm.

Smart Alec: Did you hear about the big blue monster who took first prize at Crufts?
Silly Billy: How could a monster get a prize at Crufts?
Smart Alec: He ate it.

George worked for many years as a waiter, until one day he died. His wife was quite overcome with grief and decided to try to get in touch with him through spiritualists, mediums, fortune-tellers, anyone she could find – but none of it worked.

Then one day a friend came to visit her, and when she heard about the problem she had an idea. 'I think it's quite possible that if George was haunting anywhere, he'd be haunting the restaurant where he used to work,' she suggested, 'Why don't you go there and try again?' The wife followed this advice and went to the restaurant, where she sat at a table and called for her husband to contact her.

'George, it's me,' she cried. 'Are you there?'

'Yes, I am,' whispered a ghostly voice.

'Speak louder, I can't hear you,' begged his wife.

'I can't,' came the ghostly whisper.

'Then come over to this table.'

'I can't do that,' said George's ghost. 'It's not my table.'

Did you hear about the bike that was possessed by devils and went around biting people?
It was known as the vicious cycle.

Witch: How does it feel to hurtle through doors and walls?
Ghost: It hurtles.

1st Witch: Where's your toad?
2nd Witch: He's out doing some spying for me.
1st Witch: Spying?
2nd Witch: Didn't you know? He's a croak and dagger agent.

How do monsters count to thirteen?
   On their fingers.
How do they count to forty-seven?
   They take off their socks and count their toes.

Igor: There's a ghost here to see you, sir.
Dr Frankenstein: Tell him I can't see him.

There once was an old witch called Rose,
Who had several huge warts on her nose.
So she had them removed:
Her appearance improved –
But her glasses dropped down to her toes.

Did you hear about the little spook who couldn't sleep at night because his brother kept telling him human stories?

Which ghost was president of France?
   Charles de Ghoul.

1st Ghost: Did you read in the paper about the two tribes of cannibals who went to war against each other?
2nd Ghost: Terrible, wasn't it? Apparently the winners made mincemeat of the losers.

Why did the monster eat a lightbulb?
   Because he was in need of light refreshment.

How do cannibals like their shepherd's pie made?
   With real shepherds. *

* SEE
'SMART ALEC'S
REVOLTING JOKES
FOR KIDS'.

HEY! WHAT'S THIS JOKE DOING IN THIS BOOK!

A monster raced into the doctor's surgery. 'Help me, doctor,' he cried, holding a handkerchief to the back of his neck.

'What's wrong?' cried the doctor.

'I hit the back of my neck,' said the monster.

'How did you do that?'

'I stood on a table.'

What's the difference between a deer which is being chased and a short witch?

One's a hunted stag and the other's a stunted hag.

Little Ghoul: I want to join the Boy Scouts.
Mother Ghoul: Why?
Little Ghoul: I want to learn to tie knots for nooses.

Did you hear about Dr Frankenstein's friend the plastic surgeon?
He sat on a radiator and melted.

Mummy, mummy, come quick! There's a monster in the toilet.
What's it doing?
Drinking all the water!

Did you hear about the Yorkshire lady who dressed all in white so that she would be seen by traffic on dark winter nights?
She scared fourteen people to death before she was knocked down by a snowplough.

Witch: I've just invented this potion. Want to try it?
Ghoul: What is it?
Witch: You take one sip and you tell the truth.
Ghoul: Okay, pass the bucket. Slurp . . . Yuck! It's paraffin!
Witch: And that's the truth!

Knock, knock.
Who's there?
Bet.
Bet who?
Bet you never thought you'd be eaten by a monster!

1st Witch: Did you have any luck with your advert for a husband?
2nd Witch: I got seven replies. They all said, 'You can have mine!'

Why did the Egyptian ghost worry?
  Because her mummy was a daddy.

Why did the werewolf go to the barber?
  He couldn't stand his hair any longer.

The Reverend Postlethwaite was a very famous missionary. He gave the cannibal tribesmen of Upper Oomperland their first taste of Christianity.

The wizard who'd invented a flying carpet was interviewed for the local radio station. 'What's it like, Merlin, to fly on a magic carpet?' asked the radio interviewer.
  'Rugged,' replied Merlin.

Algy met a bear.
The bear met Algy.
The bear was bulgy.
The bulge was Algy.

Monster: I've just had the bolts removed from my neck.
Ghoul: Have a scar?
Monster: No thanks, I don't smoke.

Some cowboys were sitting around a campfire late one night telling each other stories. 'I know a Red Indian who never, ever forgets anything. The Devil can have my soul if I'm lying,' boasted one.

That night the Devil, who'd been listening, appeared to the cowboy and said, 'I warn you, if you were telling a lie about that Red Indian I'll take your soul when you die.'

'I'm not,' said the cowboy. 'Come and meet him yourself.'

The two of them went to where the Indian had pitched his tepee and the Devil asked him one question. 'Do you like eggs?'

'Yes,' said the Indian. This was enough for the Devil, and he and the cowboy went off on their own separate ways. Some years later the cowboy died and the Devil collected his ghost and took it back to the Red Indian to see whether he remembered them.

'How!' said the Devil, greeting the Indian in the traditional way.

'Scrambled,' replied the Indian.

*What single word describes the spooky sight of
100 cakes doing the tango?*
  Abundance.

1st Spook: I hear you've got a new job.
2nd Spook: Yes, I've started working for a
spiritualist.
1st Spook: Is he much good?
2nd Spook: Oh, medium, I'd say.

*How do you know if there's a monster in your
custard?*
  When it's *really* lumpy.

1st Cannibal: I don't think very much of your
chef.
2nd Cannibal: Just eat the vegetables then.

Igor: Dr Frankenstein's just invented a new
kind of glue.
Dracula: I hope it doesn't make him stuck up.

Three travellers were crossing the bleak moors one night when a terrible storm blew up. Soaked to the skin and freezing, they made their way towards a dim light that flickered in the distance. When they reached it they discovered an eerie-looking house, with tall, twisted chimneys and hideous gargoyles leering down at them from the eaves. Despite their fears they knocked and the door was opened by an old crone wearing long black robes and with horrible warts all over her face.

'Come in, my dears,' she smiled, revealing that most of her teeth were missing. 'I had a feeling that you were coming.'

Nervously the travellers entered the hall, which was full of purring black cats. A bat hung upside down from the lightbulb. 'Can you put us up for the night,' stammered one of the men.

'Oh yes,' said the witch. 'But before I show you up to your beds, would you like a hot drink? Hot chocolate or coffee?'

'Hot chocolate for me, please,' said the first man.

'Coffee for me, please,' said the second man.

'I'll have hot chocolate,' said the third.

Which just goes to show that two out of three people prefer hot chocolate before they go to bed at night.

The vampire went into the Monster Café.
'Shark and chips,' he ordered.
'And make it snappy.'

1st Monster: What's that horrible green thing on your shoulders?
2nd Monster: Aaaagh! Get it off!
1st Monster: Don't panic, it's your head.

A huge hairy monster went to the doctor to ask for help because he was becoming very weak. The doctor prescribed some pills and a tonic to build him up. A few days later the monster came back to the surgery.
'Are you feeling stronger?' asked the doctor.
'No,' said the monster. 'The medicine isn't working – you see, I can't get the tops off the bottles.'

Why are most monsters covered in wrinkles?
Have you ever tried to iron a monster?

1st Monster: Have you seen my new dog? He's got no legs and I call him Cigarette.
2nd Monster: Why Cigarette?
1st Monster: I have to take him outside for a drag.

IF I WASN'T SO BUSY RUNNING AWAY FROM THE GHOST – I'D BITE THAT JOKE!

In a dim, dark lane there was a dim, dark
  house,
And in that dim, dark house there was a dim,
  dark attic,
And in that dim, dark attic there was a dim,
  dark oak chest,
And in that dim, dark oak chest there was a
  dim, dark suitcase,
And in that dim, dark suitcase there was a
  GHOST!

Where was Dracula when the lights went out?
  In the dark.

Monster: Stick 'em down!
Ghost: Don't you mean stick 'em up?
Monster: No wonder I'm not making much
money in this business.

Dr Frankenstein: With Christmas coming up,
Igor, I'm going to try a seasonal experiment
and cross an octopus with a chicken.
Igor: Why?
Dr Frankenstein: So that everyone can have a
leg for dinner.

Boris the monster knocked on a witch's door
and asked for something to eat. 'You look
familiar,' said the witch. 'Didn't I give you
some bat's blood soup last week?'
  'Yes,' said the monster, 'but I'm better
now.'

There was an old lady who had earned herself a wonderful local reputation as a weather forecaster – in fact she was so accurate that many people thought she was a witch. People came from far and wide to see her before they booked their holidays or sowed their crops. But one day there was a lot of concern because the old lady stopped making her forecasts. An old farmer, who'd always relied on her predictions, went to see her. 'Please,' he begged, 'tell me the best day to sow my wheat. You've always got the weather right before.'

'I can't,' said the old lady.

'Why?' asked the farmer. 'Have your special powers deserted you?'

'No,' said the old lady. 'My radio's broken.'

Why do monsters wear glasses?
So that they don't bump in to other monsters.

1st Ghost: My son's so stupid!
2nd Ghost: Why, what does he do?
1st Ghost: He keeps climbing walls.

Knock, knock.
Who's there?
Frank.
Frank who?
Frankenstein. ✱

✱SEE 'SMART ALEC'S KNOCK-KNOCK JOKES FOR KIDS'
YOU'LL BE KNOCKED OUT!

CLEVER JOKE
BY ME - STARVING
ARTIST

Father monster came home from the Monster Repair Company to find his son Boris in disgrace. 'He's been fighting again,' said mother monster. 'It's those terrible Slime children down the road. They're such a bad influence on him. He learned all about punching and kicking from them.'

'Yes,' interrupted Boris, 'but hitting them on the head with an axe was my own idea.'

1st Witch: I'm going to cast a spell and make myself beautiful. I'll have hundreds of men at my feet.
2nd Witch: Yes, chiropodists.

The wonderful Wizard of Oz
Retired from business becoz
What with up-to-date science
To most of his clients
He wasn't the wiz that he woz.

What do vicars write in?
  Exorcise books.

What jewels do monsters wear?
  Tombstones.

1st Cannibal: Am I too late for lunch?
2nd Cannibal: Yes, everyone's been eaten.

Why does Frankenstein's monster go click-click-click-click?
   It's just his bones knitting.

What's the difference between a lemon and a purple monster?
   A lemon is yellow.

Why did the stupid monster give up boxing?
   He didn't want to spoil his looks.

Hickory, dickory, dock,
The monster ran up the clock.
The clock is now being repaired.

It was late one night and a cyclist on the way back home had a puncture. He propped his bike up against the cemetery wall and examined the tyre, but there was nothing he could do about it – he was going to have to walk home. And the shortest route was through the cemetery. It was very dark and very creepy as he opened the gates and went in. Lightning flashed across the sky and in the distance he heard the church clock strike midnight. Suddenly he heard a strange tapping sound coming from one part of the cemetery and, despite his nervousness, he went over to see what was happening. He peered out from behind a gravestone and saw a shadowy figure all in white and holding a hammer and chisel.

'What are you doing?' asked the man nervously.

'Just correcting my headstone,' said the thing in white. 'You see, when they buried me they spelled my name wrong . . .'

Why does Count Dracula give lessons in bloodsucking to young vampires?
He likes to bring new blood into the business.

How can you spot a monster on Come Dancing?
  He's the one with three left feet.

Where do ghosts go for holidays abroad?
  The Ghosta Brava.

1st Ghost: I don't agree with you at all!
2nd Ghost: Why not?
1st Ghost: There's absolutely no evidence that people exist.

Why did the one-eyed monster give up teaching?
  What's the point with only one pupil?

There once was a doctor who lived in the house next door to one of his most awkward patients. The patient made a real nuisance of himself. If he didn't feel well during the day he'd run into the back garden and yell over the garden wall, 'Doctor, doctor, can you give me something for my tummy ache?' And if he didn't feel well in the night he'd bang on the wall, no matter what time it was, and shout, 'Doctor, doctor, can you give me something for my cold?'

Finally, after many years, the patient died. The doctor's relief didn't last long because a few days later he too died, and by an amazing coincidence they were buried side by side in the graveyard. It was quiet and still in the cemetery, and the church clock struck midnight. Suddenly the doctor heard a ghostly banging on the side of his cold, dark coffin, and a spooky voice said, 'Doctor, doctor, can you give me something for worms?'

1st Cannibal: I don't like my wife.
2nd Cannibal: Yes, you're right. A bit more pepper and some garlic would help, I think.

Why did the lady monster wear curlers at night?
   She wanted to wake up curly in the morning.

What did Tarzan say when the werewolf chewed his leg off?
Ah-eaaah-eaaah!

Little Monster: Mummy, mummy, I don't want to go to Australia!
Mummy Monster: Just shut up and keep swimming.

Ghost: I've been invited to an avoidance.
Monster: An avoidance? What's that?
Ghost: It's a dance for people who hate each other.

A cannibal chief was just about to stew his latest victim for dinner when the man protested, 'You can't eat me – I'm a manager!'
   'Well,' said the cannibal, 'Soon you'll be a manager in chief.'

Did you hear about the stupid werewolf? It lay down to chew a bone and when it got up it only had three legs.

Mrs Monster: I'd like a dress to match my eyes, please.
Shop Assistant: I don't think we've got any bloodshot yellow dresses, madam.

A salesman walked up to the front door of a house, rang the bell and, when the door opened, sprinkled dust along the path and into the hall.

'What's this?' asked the surprised housewife.

'It's ghost dust,' explained the salesman. 'You just sprinkle it on the ground and you don't suffer from ghosts.'

'But we don't have ghosts anyway,' protested the housewife.

The salesman just smiled. 'You see, it works!'

What is even more invisible than the invisible ghost?
His shadow.

Smart Alec: Something terrible just happened to the jelly monster.'
Silly Billy: What?
Smart Alec: It set.

1st Witch: I bought one of those new paper cauldrons they've been advertising on the TV.
2nd Witch: What's it like?
1st Witch: Tearable.

Why is the letter T so important to the sticky monster?
Because without it he'd be the sicky monster.

A monster walked into a music shop and asked the owner for a mouth organ. 'This is extraordinary,' exclaimed the owner. 'Only this morning I had another monster in here asking for a mouth organ. In all my years in this shop I've never had even *one* monster buy a mouth organ and now there have been two of you in a single day. It's incredible.'
'Yes,' smiled the monster. 'The other one must have been Armonica.'

What did Dr Frankenstein get when he crossed a monster with a mouse?
    Huge holes in the skirting board.

How do ghosts keep fit?
    By regular exorcise.

Why are werewolves like playing cards?
    Because they come in packs.

What did the monster say when he found he had only thistles to eat?
    Thistle have to do.

What do witches yell when they're riding in the sky?
    'Broom-Broom'.

A human being once walked into the Monster Café by mistake, bought a cup of tea and sat down. Halfway through his cuppa he noticed a werewolf watching him from a nearby table. The werewolf began to growl.

'Is he safe?' asked the man nervously.

'Well,' said the waiter, 'he's a lot safer than you are.'

How many monsters can you cram into an empty coffin?

Only one – after that it isn't empty any more.

Three very old and rather deaf monsters met in the park. 'It's windy today, isn't it?' said one.

'No, it's Thursday,' said the other.

'So am I,' said the third. 'Let's all go and have a cup of tea.'

What delivers monsters' babies?

A Frankenstork.

And what gift did the monsters give to baby Jesus?

Frankencense.

1st Witch: Shall I buy red or black candles? Which burn longer?
2nd Witch: They both burn shorter.

How do monsters dress on a cold day?
   Quickly.

1st Cannibal: Does your wife cook best by gas or electricity?
2nd Cannibal: I don't know, I've never tried cooking her.

Why won't Count Dracula eat in restaurants?
   He's worried about getting a steak through the heart.

Count Dracula went to visit a friend of his, a vampire who had just had most of his teeth removed and was now left with just one, in the middle of his gums. 'Tell me,' asked Dracula, 'how do you cope with only one tooth?'
   'I just grin and bare it,' said the vampire.

Frankenstein's Monster: I've changed my mind.
Dr Frankenstein: Let's hope this new one works better than the old one did.

Epilaugh:
   Here lie the bones of Richard Lawton,
Whose death, alas! was strangely brought on.
Trying one day his corns to mow off,
The razor slipped and cut his toe off.
His toe, or rather, what it grew to,
An inflammation quickly flew to,
Which took, alas, to mortifying.
And that was the cause of Richard's dying.

Spook: I went to the graveyard today.
Phantom: Someone dead?
Spook: Yes, all of them.

Why did the mummy never catch cold?
   She was always well wrapped up.

Mary had a bionic cow,
It lived on safety pins.
And every time she milked that cow
The milk came out in tins.

Why do monsters eat raw meat?
No one taught them how to cook.

Did you hear about a competition to find the laziest spook in the world? All the competitors were lined up on stage. 'I've got a really nice, easy job for the laziest person here,' said the organizer. 'Will the laziest spook raise his hand?'

All the spooks put their hands up – except one. 'Why didn't you raise your arm?' asked the presenter.

'Too much bother,' yawned the spook.

How do witches like to drink their tea?
From a cup and sorceror.

Would you say that Dracula movies are fangtastic?

Two monsters were working on a building site. When lunchtime came one of them took out a box of sandwiches. 'Rat paste and tomato,' he moaned as he bit into the first. 'More rat paste and tomato,' he muttered as he ate the second.

'Rat paste and tomato?' asked his friend as he picked up the third sandwich.

'Yes,' sighed the monster. 'I hate rat paste and tomato.'

'Why don't you ask your wife to make you something different?'

The monster looked at him strangely. 'I don't have a wife – I make my sandwiches myself.'

Mummy, mummy, who don't we buy a dustbin for our rubbish?

Shut up and keep eating.

Why did the monster take a dead man for a drive in his car?

Because he was a car-case.

THERE'S THAT STUPID SOCK!

A little boy had been to play with one of his friends for the evening and stayed rather late. 'Why not stay here for the night?' suggested the friend's mother. 'We have a spare room. Come up and see.' The boy followed her up the stairs and into a gloomy-looking bedroom. In the middle of one wall was a door.

'Where does that go?' he asked.

'That goes no-where,' said his friend's mother. 'You must promise me that, whatever happens, you'll never try to open that door. Do you understand? You must never, ever open than door.'

Naturally the boy agreed, but he couldn't seem to take his eyes off the door as he got undressed and climbed into bed. Finally, forgetting what had been said, he crept out of bed and slowly pulled open the door. With a creak it opened, and the boy peered into the dark, musty-smelling room beyond. A few feet away something seemed to be moving – something shiny and slithery, which made a tapping noise as it crossed the floor in his direction. . . . Something cold and creepy, with two horrible green eyes that were watching *him*! With a cry of horror the boy raced out of the bedroom and onto the landing – and with a horrible, slithering sound, the *thing* followed.

Terrified, the boy ran downstairs and threw open the front door, then raced into the night, and all the time that horrible, slimy, rasping, nightmarish *thing* came after him. At the end of the garden was a river with a boat, and he jumped into it and began to row across, hoping, praying, that the *thing* wouldn't be able to follow him. And it didn't, because when he looked back across the river he couldn't see it anywhere. With relief he pulled the boat in to the opposite bank and sat there on the grass panting and getting his breath back. And as he sat there a horrible slimy tentacle crept out of the water, followed by the dripping *thing*, which stared at him with its hideous green eyes. 'Got you,' it hissed wickedly, and its tentacle tapped him clammily on the knee. 'Now *you're* it!'

What does Dracula say to his victims?
   It's been nice gnawing you.

What should you do if a zombie borrows your comic?
   Wait for him to give it back.

A ghost stood on the bridge one night,
Its lips were all a-quiver.
It gave a cough,
Its head fell off,
And floated down the river.

What should you call a nervous witch?
   A twitch.

Did you hear about the skeleton which was attacked by a dog?
It ran off with some bones and left him without a leg to stand on.

Knock, knock.
Who's there?
Dismay.
Dismay who?
Dismay come as a surprise – I've come to eat you!

Did you hear about the Irish monster who wore all his clothes to paint his house because the label on the tin said, 'Put on three coats'?

Why did the monster take his nose apart?
   To see what made it run.

Frankenstein's Monster: They can't do my transplant this week, Dr Frankenstein doesn't have a bed free.
Igor: You'll just have to keep talking about your old operation then, won't you?

Where do ghouls go for holidays?
   Wails.

What happened after the monster ate Les Dawson?
   He felt funny.

Baby Ghost: Mummy, mummy, am I a real ghost?
Mummy Ghost: Of course you are.
Baby Ghost: Are you absolutely sure?
Mummy Ghost: Of course I am. Why?
Baby Ghost: Because I hate the dark!

Why do demons get on so well with ghouls?
   Because demons are a ghoul's best friend.

1st Ghost: I'm finding it a real bore haunting this dungeon these days.

2nd Ghost: Me too – I just can't put any life into it.

What did the undertaker say to his girlfriend?
  'Em-balmy about you.'

Did you hear about the spook who went to have a haircut? 'I'm busy,' said the barber. 'You'll have to wait.'
  'That's okay,' said the ghost. 'I'll leave me head here and call back for it later.'

A monster decided to become a TV star, so he went to see an agent. 'What do you do? asked the agent.
  'Bird impressions,' said the monster.
  'What kind of bird impressions?'
  'I eat worms.'

Spooky happenings at the supermarket! A customer was just leaning over the freezer looking for some frozen chips when ten fish fingers crept up and pulled him in . . .

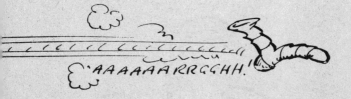

'AAAAAARRGGHH.'

It was Hallowe'en and the phantom police were on the lookout for any witches riding on their broomsticks without proper care and attention. As they watched the sky they were horrified to see a witch whiz past knitting. 'Pull over!' they called as they overtook her.

'No,' she replied, 'a pair of socks.'

Igor: Only this morning Dr Frankenstein completed another amazing operation.
He crossed an ostrich with a centipede.
Dracula: And what did he get?
Igor: We don't know – we haven't managed to catch it yet.

Why do monsters carry umbrellas?
Because umbrellas can't walk.

After years of travelling around the world in his search, the wicked Abanazar finally discovered the enchanted cave in which he believed lay the magic lamp which would make him millions. He stood before the boulders which sealed the cave and uttered the magic words, 'Open Sesame!' There was silence, and then a ghostly voice from within moaned, 'Open says-a who?'

Why is a stupid monster like the Amazon jungle?
Because they're both dense.

1st Monster: I went for a swim in the sea last summer and a shark bit off my leg.
2nd Monster: Which one?
1st Monster: No idea, they all look the same to me.

Two burglars broke into a witch's house, hoping to steal some of her magic potions. However, they'd just crept into the hallway when they heard the witch's voice saying, 'First I'm going to nibble your arms. Then I'm going to bite off your feet. Next I'm going to eat your head . . .'
With a scream of terror the two burglars fled. 'What was that?' said the witch, putting down her bag of jelly babies . . .

Did you hear the joke about the monster who climbed Nelson's Column?
Funny, neither did I . . .

Who haunted the graveyard when the spooks went on strike?
The skeleton staff.

What should you call an admiral's ghost?
A seal ghoul.

Why are storytellers like monsters?
Because their tales come out of their heads.

Why do monsters have fur coats?
They'd look silly in plastic macs, wouldn't they?

Did you hear about Smart Alec's grandfather? It wasn't his cough that carried him off, it was the coffin they carried him off in.

Smart Alec: There's 2 monsters who serves at our local greengrocer's shop.
He's 8 feet tall and 60 inches wide. Can you guess what he weighs?
Silly Billy: No.
Smart Alec: Vegetables.

Two monsters were out for some fresh air when one of them was run over by a lorry. 'Don't just stand there, call me an ambulance!' he cried as he lay on the ground with all five feet waving in the air.
'All right,' said his friend. 'If it makes you feel any better, you're an ambulance!'

Did you hear about the giant monster who went shoplifting?
He got squashed under Sainsburys.

Dracula and Frankenstein's monster were stranded out in the countryside after Dracula's hearse broke down. They were ambling along a lane, picking wild flowers and wondering how many miles they were going to have to walk when a motorist in a Mini passed them and stopped. 'I can give you a lift if you like,' he told Dracula, 'but I don't have room for your big friend.'

'That's all right,' said Dracula, climbing in. 'He'll follow us.' Off went the Mini, with the driver purposely keeping the speed down to give the monster a chance to keep up. Frankenstein trotted behind without any trouble, so the car speeded up to forty and then fifty miles an hour. Still the monster ran behind without any trouble. The driver was amazed, and then he became alarmed as he noticed that Frankenstein's monster was poking his tongue out of the right side of his mouth.

'Perhaps I'd better stop,' he suggested. 'Your friend's tongue is poking out.'

'Don't worry,' said Dracula. 'It means he's going to overtake.'

Why did the little monster get into trouble for feeding the monkeys at the zoo?
He fed them to the lions.

1st Witch: How old are you?
2nd Witch: One hundred and nine – but I don't look it, do I?
1st Witch: No, but you used to.

What do you get if you cross an Abominable Snowman with a footballer?
I don't know, but when it tries to score a goal no one stops it.

1st Ghoul: That girl over there looks like Helen Green.
2nd Ghoul: She looks even worse in blue.

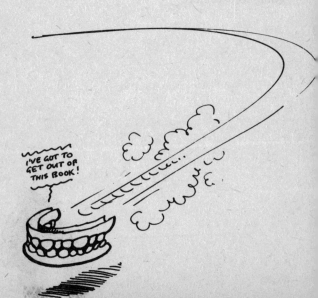

I'VE GOT TO GET OUT OF THIS BOOK!

Two monsters were watching TV when Madonna appeared wearing nothing but a sexy black swimsuit. 'Hmm,' said one monster turning to the other, 'if I ever give up hating human beings I think she's the one I'd stop hating first.'

1st Monster: Why have you tied a knot in your neck?
2nd Monster: I didn't want my cold to go to my chest.

'Who's been eating my worms in slime?' asked father monster.
   'Who's been eating my minced cockroaches in diesel oil?' asked baby monster.
   'Stop complaining both of you,' yelled mother monster. 'I haven't made breakfast yet.'

A monster went shopping with sponge-fingers in one ear and jelly and custard in the other.

'Why have you got jelly and custard and sponge in your ears?' asked the shop assistant.

'You'll have to speak up,' said the monster. 'I'm a trifle deaf.'

What did the wizard say on the last day of the world?

'Armageddon out of here.'

Did you hear about the utterly brainless monster who sat on the floor?
He fell off.

Teacher: Boris, where are the pyramids?
Boris: I don't know.
Teacher: Well where did you put them?

What happened when the Ice Monster ate a curry?

He blew his cool.

What do you call a sorceress who stops cars with her thumb?
   A witch hiker.

1st Ghost: I'm going to France tomorrow.
2nd Ghost: By ferry?
1st Ghost: No – by hovercraft, of course!

Once upon a time there was a very ugly monster who lived a lonely, unhappy life. He longed for company, so one day he got up the courage to put an advert in the newspaper for a girlfriend. A lady did reply, and they wrote to each other several times before they decided that it was time to meet.

   'I must warn you that I'm not very good-looking,' wrote the monster nervously. 'In fact I have four heads, I'm covered in nasty yellow scabs, and I've got clumps of green hair growing all over me. I also have two wooden legs and one of my arms trails along the ground when I walk. If, having heard this, you still want to meet me, I suggest we meet under the clock at King's Cross on Saturday at three.'

   A couple of days later a letter came from the lady. The monster opened it with trembling fingers, terrified that his description would have put her off. 'I think personality is more important than looks,' he read, 'so I look forward to meeting you on Saturday. Would you wear a pink carnation so that I can recognize you?'

Doctor, doctor, I keep thinking I'm a ghost!
I expect that's why you just walked through that wall.

Why did the ghost's trousers fall down?
Because he had no visible means of support.

What do ghosts call the spooky navy?
The Ghost Guard.

What's the difference between a vampire and a matterbaby?
What's a matterbaby?
Nothing – what's wrong with you?

Two people went into a very dark, spooky cave. 'I can't see a thing,' said one.
'Hold my hand,' said the other.
'All right.' The first man reached out. 'Take off that horrible bristly glove first, though.'
'But I'm not wearing a glove . . .'

Igor: Is there any difference between lightning and electricity?
Dr Frankenstein: Have you ever seen a lightning bill?

What steps should you take if you're out late at night and you're followed by a thirsty vampire?
   Very big ones.

Why did the monster jump up and down?
   Because he'd just taken his medicine and he'd forgotten to shake the bottle.

'You're so ugly,' said Dracula to the witch when they were in the pub one night.
   'And you're drunk,' replied the witch.
   'Yes,' said Dracula. 'But in the morning I'll be sober.'

Did you hear about the ghost who lives in Westminster?
He's just been made spooker of the House of Lords.

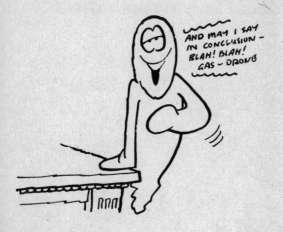

AND MAY I SAY
IN CONCLUSION —
BLAH! BLAH!
GAS — DRONE

Epitaph on a gravestone:
My husband's dead and here he lies.
Nobody laughs and nobody cries.
Where he's gone or how he fares,
Nobody knows and nobody cares.

Why did the ghost leave his grave after 500 years?
    He felt he was old enough to leave home.

What happens to witches when it rains?
    They get wet.

Which murderous Victorian monster lives at the bottom of the sea?
    Jack the Kipper.

1st Vampire: Will you join me in a glass of tomato juice?
2nd Vampire: I don't think there's room for two in there.

Little Cannibal: I've been out hunting with my dad.
Ghoul: Catch anything?
Little Cannibal: Yes, two tourists, a missionary and a potfer.
Ghoul: What's a potfer?
Little Cannibal: To cook them in, of course.

A ghoul walked into the Monster Café and ordered a knickerbocker glory in a tall glass. When the waitress brought it to him he spooned the ice-cream out onto the floor and began to tuck into the glass. 'Yum, yum,' he said, licking his lips and putting the knobbly glass stem on the side of his plate.

A ghost who had been watching all this came over. 'What do you think you're doing?' he asked in annoyance.

'I don't like ice cream,' explained the ghoul, 'but I love glass.'

'I understand that,' said the ghost, picking up the glass stem from the plate, 'But why are you leaving the best bit?'

Igor: There's a question I'd like to ask you, Count Dracula.
Dracula: Go ahead.
Igor: Why do you always chew mints?
Dracula: Strictly between you and me, Igor, I suffer from bat breath.

Monster: I'm going to have to stop going out with that dragon.

Ghost: Why? He's hot stuff.

Monster: I know, but every time we kiss he steams my glasses up.

Two old ladies were looking at a mummy on display in the British Museum. '1000 BC,' read one of them aloud, looking at the sign on the case. 'What does that mean?'

'I expect it's the number of the car that ran him over,' said the other.

Dr Frankenstein: How did you get that splinter in your finger?

Monster: I scratched my head.

Which spook pulls horrid faces at Han Solo and Luke Skywalker?

Princess Leer.

Two villains heard that an old lady had just died and been buried in the churchyard, and that a very valuable diamond ring had been buried with her on her finger. They decided to open the grave and dig it up, and this gruesome task they completed. But try as they might they couldn't remove the beautiful ring from her finger. 'I'll have to chop her finger off,' said one of the robbers, and he did.

When they'd finished their horrible task they looked around for somewhere to spend the night before they made their escape. The only place seemed to be a very big, eerie old house with a sign up offering Bed and Breakfast. They went up the front steps and knocked, and a hideous old lady opened the door and let them in. 'Would you like a hot drink before you go to bed?' she asked them.

'Oh yes,' they said, and followed her into a dusty old kitchen. As she poured them a cup of tea they noticed that she had one finger missing. 'How did you lose your finger?' one of the villains asked curiously.

The old lady seemed to flicker before their eyes, and she turned a terrible red-eyed gaze on them. 'It was cut off,' she moaned, 'and you've got it in your pocket . . .'

How do monsters dress on a cold day?
  Quickly.

Monster: You've got a simple choice. Give me your money or I'll eat you up.
Smart Alec: You'd better eat me – I'm saving my money for my old age.

What do you call an Irishman who is dug up after 100 years?
   Pete.

Where do you find monster snails?
   At the end of monster's fingers.

What's huge and hairy and red and hides in corners?
   An embarrassed monster.

Why do sorcerors drink lots of tea?
   Because sorcerors need cuppas.

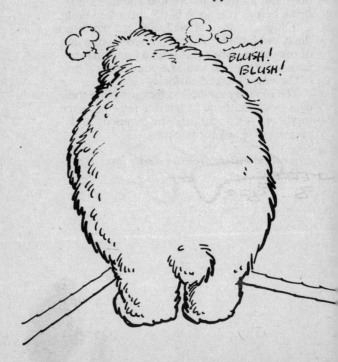

BLUSH!
BLUSH!

What do green, hairy-bottomed monsters have that no one else has?
   Baby green, hairy-bottomed monsters.

1st Cannibal: My husband's always moaning.
2nd Cannibal: So is mine. To hear him go on you'd think he already had one foot in the gravy.

Knock, knock.
   Who's there?
Ammonia.
   Ammonia who?
Ammonia little vampire and I can't reach the bell.

Why are ghouls always poor?
   Because a ghoul and his money are soon parted.

What kind of mistakes do spooks make?
   Boo-boos.

Smart Alec: What's green and shiny, has yellow fangs, little red eyes and twenty purple hairy legs?

Silly Billy: I don't know. What is it?

Smart Alec: I don't know either, but there's one crawling up your leg.

Why couldn't Dracula's wife get to sleep?
   Because of his coffin.

A sea monster who saw an oil tanker,
Munched a hole in the side and then sank her.
It swallowed the crew
In a minute or two,
And then picked its teeth with the anchor.

What is the monsters' favourite ballet?
   Swamp Lake.

Who appears on the front of ghostly magazines?
   The cover ghoul.

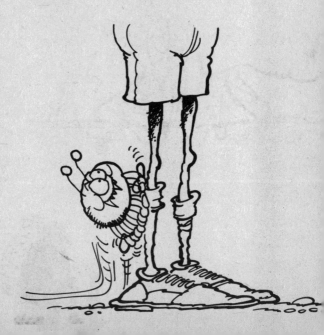

Why do mummies make excellent spies?
   They're good at keeping things under wraps.

A young man of chill Aberdeen,
Once grew so remarkably lean,
So flat and compressed,
That his back touched his chest,
And sideways he couldn't be seen.

Ghoul Nurse: How many patients has Dr Frankenstein seen this afternoon?
   Two?
Ghost Nurse: No, three. I've taken them all to the morgue.

Why did the skeleton refuse to go to the cinema?
   Because his heart wasn't in it.

The undertaker and his assistants were trying to load a coffin containing a dead monster into the hearse. As the monster was 3 metres long it was very difficult. They staggered down the steps, got one end into the car, but just as they'd wedged the coffin almost in place one of the assistants let go and it fell to the floor. 'This is no good,' said the undertaker. 'We'll have to re-hearse it now!'

1st Witch: A werewolf bit me on the leg last night.
2nd Witch: Did you put anything on it?
1st Witch: No, it must have tasted okay as it was.

What did the monster do when his wife turned into a pillar of salt?
  He put her in the cellar.

What is black and has eight wheels?
  A witch on roller skates.

What soup do Irish cannibals like best?
  The broth of a boy.

Monster: Do you have many church bells in Paris?
Hunchback of Notre Dame: About two hundred, all tolled.

What's 30 metres tall and goes 'eef, if, of, muf?'
  A backward giant.

Why did the huge horrible monster go to see the psychiatrist?
  Because he was worried that people liked him.

1st Witch: I'm terribly sorry. I just cast the wrong spell and I turned your black cat into an elephant. Can I replace him?
2nd Witch: Are you any good at catching mice?

How do monsters pass through locked doors?
   They use skeleton keys.

What shows do ghosts go to at Christmas?
   Phantomimes.

Smart Alec: I just bought a haunted bicycle.
Silly Billy: How do you know it's haunted?
Smart Alec: It's got lots of spooks in its wheels.